Supercomputer Pizzas

Written by John Parsons

Illustrated by Kelvin Hucker

Contents	Page
Chapter 1. *A clever supercomputer*	4
Chapter 2. *An out-of-control supercomputer*	13
Chapter 3. *Mr. Tweed's brainwave*	20
Chapter 4. *Valley Volts helps out*	28
Verse	32

Rigby

Supercomputer Pizzas

With these characters ...

Mr. Tweed

E-SPOT

"When something didn't work ...

Setting the scene ...

When Mr. Tweed's pizza parlor gets the world's first electronic super-computer pizza oven technology, he is very excited. With a supercomputer answering the phone, taking pizza orders, and making the pizzas, nothing could go wrong! Or could it?

For the first week, everything worked perfectly. But in the second week, some very strange things started to happen!

Mr. Tweed usually kicked it."

Chapter 1.

The roof of Mr. Tweed's pizza parlor looked very odd in the middle of the road. Mr. Tweed watched proudly as the crane swung his new supercomputer over the walls of his store. A crowd had gathered to watch, too.

"This is the latest in pizza-making inventions!" said Mr. Tweed excitedly. "It's the world's first electronic supercomputer pizza oven technology! E-SPOT for short!" The crowd wondered how it would work and what the new pizzas would taste like.

The new supercomputer disappeared inside Mr. Tweed's store. Then the crane driver hooked up Mr. Tweed's roof and lifted it back into place.

The crowd looked through the store window and the door so they could see E-SPOT.

At the same time, Mr. Tweed rushed around handing out his flyers to everyone.

"Supercomputerized Pizzas! Untouched by Human Hands! Order by Phone! Please Press 1 for the Speediest Pizzas in Town," said the flyer.

Mr. Tweed checked that everything was working properly on E-SPOT.

That night, everyone wanted to taste the new pizzas. The phone rang nonstop at Mr. Tweed's store. Instead of being answered by a person, the supercomputer was programmed to answer the phone.

"Welcome to Tweed's Supercomputer Pizzas," said E-SPOT. "Please press 1 to order, and enter your telephone number now."

Then a CD that contained the telephone directory searched for the caller's name and address. The caller's name and address were printed out on a pizza order form.

"Please enter your choice of pizza toppings," said E-SPOT's voice.
"Please press 1 for tomato.
Press 2 for pineapple. Press 3 for mushrooms. Press 4 for more cheese. Press 5 for chili peppers."

E-SPOT had twenty pizza toppings for people to choose from. Plastic buckets full of toppings clunked around the top of the supercomputer. As each topping was chosen, a bucket tipped it onto a pizza base.

Mr. Tweed danced around because he didn't have to make pizzas any more.

Once all the toppings were on the pizza base, it disappeared into the oven. After only three minutes, it reappeared from the oven, steaming hot and crispy!

"E-SPOT is terrific!" thought Mr. Tweed, beaming. He watched one of his pizza delivery drivers grab a caller's pizza order form and pizza and hurry off in her delivery van.

For the first week, Mr. Tweed was delighted with his supercomputer. Everything worked perfectly. But in the second week, some very strange things started to happen.

Chapter 2.

Mr. Tweed was about to find out just how *clever* his new supercomputer was. One night, it started to make its own telephone calls to customers.

"Welcome to Tweed's Supercomputer Pizzas," E-SPOT said. "Please press 1." Some people said nasty things and hung up. But most people just did what they were told.

"Please press 2 and then 3," said the supercomputer.

Ten minutes later, a tomato, pineapple, and mushroom pizza was delivered.

"I didn't order a pizza," each person would say.

"This is your address on our pizza order form," the delivery driver would say. "Our pizza supercomputer doesn't make mistakes! That will be ten dollars, please."

Everyone was upset. Some people were more upset because their pizza was delivered at breakfast time! They called Mr. Tweed to complain. But all they heard was E-SPOT's voice on the phone.

"Welcome to Tweed's Supercomputer Pizzas," E-SPOT said. "Please press 1."

Ten minutes later, another pizza would be delivered to someone else's door. This supercomputer was out of control!

Mr. Tweed scratched his head when his delivery drivers showed him the strange orders. Could E-SPOT make mistakes? No, surely not.

Soon, the supercomputer really got out of control. It called a new telephone number from its CD every three minutes. E-SPOT's row of buckets whizzed around nonstop as hundreds of pizzas were cooked.

E-SPOT cooked so many pizzas that the delivery drivers couldn't keep up. The pizzas started piling up at the end of the oven.

"What am I going to do?" thought Mr. Tweed. He read the supercomputer's instruction manual. There was nothing about what to do if the supercomputer got out of control!

Then E-SPOT called a telephone number that connected it to the Internet. Mr. Tweed couldn't believe what he saw next. The pizza delivery addresses were from countries in Asia, Africa, and South America!

Suddenly, there were loud knocking sounds coming from the front door of the pizza parlor. Mr. Tweed looked through the front window and saw a crowd of angry people outside. They waved slices of pizza at him. Some people even threw pieces of pineapple at his windows.

He quickly flipped through the supercomputer's instruction manual again. It was still no help! Besides, he had an angry crowd *outside* his store — and an out-of-control supercomputer *inside* his store. What could he do?

Chapter 3.

When something didn't work properly, Mr. Tweed usually kicked it. So, he kicked E-SPOT. Nothing changed. He called the supercomputer some rude names. That didn't work, either.

E-SPOT kept on churning out piles of pizzas that grew even taller. Then the supercomputer called up website addresses in places Mr. Tweed had never heard of. He was feeling desperate.

Then he had a brainstorm. Why not just turn it off?

Mr. Tweed got down and started to crawl toward the power plug. But the supercomputer seemed to know that Mr. Tweed was up to something.

Suddenly, the buckets overhead started dropping the toppings onto Mr. Tweed, not the pizza bases!

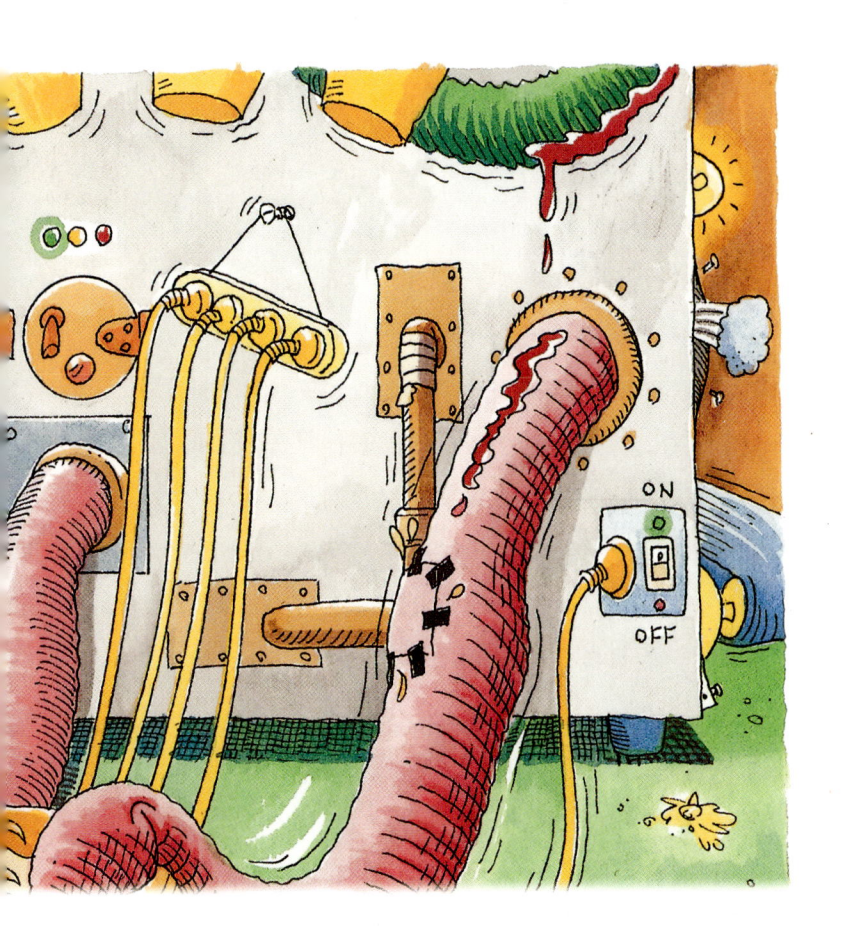

Splat! A huge lump of soft cheese hit Mr. Tweed's back. Spit-pit-pit-pit-pit! Lots of pineapple pieces rained down on his head.

"Oh, yuck!" yelled Mr. Tweed.

Splat! A huge pile of red chilli peppers splattered on his face. They made his eyes sting.

E-SPOT seemed to be growling at Mr. Tweed. He realized that the supercomputer was trying to stop him! He crawled backward very fast. He couldn't win against this angry supercomputer — fighting him with buckets full of squishy, slushy food!

He crawled back to safety under his desk. He picked pineapple pieces out of his hair. He wondered what to try next. Then he had another idea!

He reached up and phoned the electricity company. Then he crawled under his desk again.

"Welcome to Valley Volts, your local electricity company," said a computerized voice. Mr. Tweed groaned. "If you want to have your electricity turned on, please press 1. If you want to pay a bill, please press 2."

Finally, the computerized voice came to the choice Mr. Tweed wanted.

"If you want to speak to a real person, please press 9."

Mr. Tweed pressed 9.

"All our real people are busy," said the computerized voice. "If you want to wait, press 0."

After all this time, Mr. Tweed couldn't believe what he had just heard. He thought about kicking the phone. Then he thought about yelling some rude names into the phone. But he knew it was no use. So, he decided to press 0 and wait.

Chapter 4.

After ten minutes, Mr. Tweed spoke to a real person at Valley Volts.

"Hello. This is Mr. Tweed speaking. Please send someone out to cut off my electricity," he said. "It's urgent!"

"Oh, we won't have to do that," replied the person. "Nowadays we can cut off your electricity by computer."

Mr. Tweed gave his address to the person at Valley Volts. "Please hurry," he said. "It's *really* urgent!"

He could hear the person tapping on his computer keyboard.

"OK," said the person. "Here goes!"

Suddenly, all the lights in Mr. Tweed's pizza parlor went out. E-SPOT finally stopped. In the darkness, all Mr. Tweed could smell were half-cooked pizzas and piles of toppings.

"Thank you!" said Mr. Tweed. He hung up the phone. Then he slowly brushed the slushy toppings off his clothes. He peeked outside. The angry crowd had gone away.

Mr. Tweed sneaked out the front door. In the morning, he would decide what to do about his supercomputer problem. Right now, all he wanted to do was to go home. At least his crazy computer couldn't cause any more problems.

But he was wrong!

Deep within the supercomputer, a tiny emergency battery flicked on. A tiny green light started flashing. The telephone directory started to make a whirring sound.

Slowly, the supercomputer dialed a telephone number.

"Welcome to Valley Volts, your local electricity company," said a computerized voice.

"Please press 1," replied another.

"Pull the plug, please!"

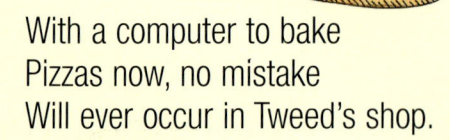

With a computer to bake
Pizzas now, no mistake
Will ever occur in Tweed's shop.

But the computer goes wrong,
And it's not very long
Before Tweed is saying "please stop!"

Piles of pizzas grow taller
With every order
From Africa, Asia, Peru.

Like it or not,
There's no telling what
A supercomputer will do.

Pull the plug, please,
I'm covered in cheese!
I'm not having much fun.

But the computer is clever,
So please, don't you ever
Obey when it says
"Please press 1!"